Be Careful of Falling Rocks

By Patrick Mooney

Copyright © 2020 Patrick Mooney
All rights reserved. No part of this publication may be reproduced, stored or transmitted in any form by any means, electronic, mechanical, photocopying or otherwise, without the prior written permission of the publisher or author.

First published in Great Britain in 2020 by Sleepy Lion Publishing
(Imprint of Sleepy Lion Limited)

Text Copyright © Patrick Mooney, 2020

Cover Illustration Copyright © Sleepy Lion Limited 2020

The right of Patrick Mooney to be identified as author of this work has been asserted by him in accordance with the Copyright, Designs and Patents Act, 1988.

ISBN: 978-1-8380152-3-7

www.sleepylionpublishing.com

Also by Patrick Mooney:

In a Word (2013 poetry book)

Down on the Lake (2019 Children's book)

Dedicated to my parents

Contents

The Anniversary	1
Cuddles	3
Memoirs from a Teddy Bear	5
The Teddy Bear Collection & First Steps	6
Valentine Weekend	11
The Kiss	13
The Connection (The Spark)	14
'Old friends make the best friends' init	15
Good Luck, No Luck, Any Luck Will Do	15
Super Saturday 2015 (Six Nations / Part 2)	17
I Love Pubs	19
One Pint of Dark, One Pint of Black and One Pint of Stout	21
Dazzo the Dazzler	24
The Pleasure of Smoking	26
Sirens	30
One Day Summer Holiday	32
The Four Seasons	34
River Carnival (2016)	37
The Day I met Benjamin	38
A Matter of Honour	40
Thunderstone	43
Coming Home	45
Too Soon	47

Touch and Feel What is Real?	49
One Thousand and Out	50
Brothers in Arms	51
Street Underground Performance	52
The Story Of The Song	56
Gravy Rap (No More Gravy)	58
Grand Ma Mooney's Irish Coddle	60
Blanket	62
Invisible Body & Lost Soul	64
Ghost Train	66
Looking on from the Outside	68
The Cowboy Within the Boy	70
No More Fear	72
One Day	72
Solitude	73
Special Day	74
Emptiness	74
Regret	75
Super Sat 2019 / Six Nations – Part 3	76
The Weeping Window	78
Saturday Night	80
Retirement	83
Racing Against Time	86
Compliment (Dedicated to my dad)	87

The Anniversary

(Dedicated to my Parents)

It was the year, nineteen hundred and sixty-three,
As they started married life in black and white,
A sheet of pureness covered the ground,
You are now man and wife.

> As everyone stood still to take some snaps,
> The blanket of white started to melt,
> With the winter sun rebounding from the ground,
> Everyone stood still.

Black and white was all they could capture,
As these were the days before Technicolor,
Handheld cameras loaded with film,
To take the perfect shot.

> For better or worse, through highs and lows,
> In sickness and in health,
> The newlyweds committed,
> To love, honour and obey each other.

Three boys they have raised,
Into men they have developed,
Grandchildren by their side,
Keeping them smiling and young at heart.

> On the fifth of January, twenty hundred and thirteen,
> Fifty golden years to the day,
> Life has come full circle and
> Developed into wide screen, high definition colour.

They remain true to each other,
As the family all grown up,
Reach for their mobile phones and digital cameras,
While Paddy and Josie sit side by side.

Reunited with all their slides,
Of the past and present,
Memories taken at a moment in time,
Will live on…lasting forever.

Cuddles

(For Little Sam)

Cuddles come fast and cuddles come slow,

Cuddles from tiny hands reaching out to hold you,

Cuddles are a friendly way of saying that I care about you,

Cuddles can be for happy or sad occasions,

Cuddles can be slight or they can be tall,

Cuddles can be strong or they can be soft,

Cuddles can be for welcoming or goodbyes,

Cuddles, cuddles, cuddles,

Saying that I love you, admire you; I am here for you,

Quaint cuddles, big bear cuddles,

Soft cuddles, strong cuddles,

Wrap you in my arms & hold you tight cuddles,

Friendly cuddles, family cuddles,

Personal cuddles, half cuddles,

Cuddles for high praise,

Cuddles for weeping,

A cuddle for your teddy bear,

A special cuddle for little Sammy,

A cuddle a day keeps the doctor away.

A Collection for Children of all ages.

(Sonnet)

Memoirs from a Teddy Bear

I came to you in the year sixty-five,
I was already two years and you brand new,
The year only nine days old, when you arrived,
Sleeping soundly, dreaming sweet dreams anew.

I lay beside you throughout the whole night,
You were so tiny, light and dressed in blue,
You cuddled me tight, it felt so right,
We were both the same size then, how time flew.

Do you remember touching my soft fur?
You named me your golden teddy bear,
So many years ago, it's become a blur,
When I lived in your favourite chair.

My green jersey has faded with lost time,
Memories help my golden fur, stay divine.

The Teddy Bear collection & First Steps

Part 1:

You took me to the woods, where I liked to climb the trees,
You took me to the beach, where I liked to play in the sand,
You took me to the park, where I liked to be pushed on the swings,
You took me to playgroup, where I liked to be held by your friends,
You took me shopping, where I liked to sit, facing you from the cart,
You took me to the swimming pool, where I watched you from the side,
You took me to birthday parties, where I kept an eye on the cake,
You took me on holiday, where we both played by the lake,
You took me to bed, where we slept soundly all night,

You cuddled me tightly, so I wouldn't fall.

You now hold me in your memories, as the fondest of them all.

Part 2:

One, two, three, four, five, six, seven, eight, nine and …teddy bear counting to ten…coming to find you…if you're ready or not…

Teddy bear, hiding in the den…or behind the door…high above…out of sight, watching you don't fall…

Teddy bear, on the top of the swings...climbing frame is well out of sight...down the slide, here I go...catch me if you can...

Teddy bear, high...teddy bear low...teddy bear everywhere...don't we know...

Teddy bear, jumping high...landing softly...hiding in the bushes...running along the fields...climbing the trees...the tree house, a favourite of ours, all the time...

Teddy bear, playing in the sand, building sandcastles that are so grand...

Teddy bear, swimming in the sea...teddy bear surfing waves so high, they can almost reach the sky...

Teddy bear, swimming with the seals...watching from the rocks overhead...rock climbing...don't mind if we do...

Teddy bear, walking along the sand...collecting shells and beautiful bright stones to take home...
Teddy bear, taking in a coastal walk...so high, he can see afar along the blue ocean sky...

Teddy bear, eating his favourite ice cream, while resting in a deck chair...

Teddy bear, washing away all the sand, from a lovely day on the beach...

Teddy bear, with sleepy eyes...pulls his blanket up tightly around his little body, all snug for the night...

Teddy bear, dreaming about tomorrow and what a new special day will bring.

Part 3:

You named me Bertie, as you received me when you were only three,
Thirty years to the day, as you play with your own child of three,
You pass me down along the years, I have counted my blessings and
Just hope that the little one looks after me, on the count of thirty-three.

One, three, thirty, who's counting, not me, as I look to the child in front of me,
To take me by her side and treasure me, as you once did and continue to do so,
I know that you will always remember me, as I will you,
Memories last forever, as our special love will continue.

First Steps

Part 1:

First steps, from shaking, wiggling, crawling,
Harry is one year old today,
Twelve months, fifty two weeks and
Three hundred and sixty five days.

Harry has seen Max, his older brother by two years
Thinking, that I'm not staying still for long?

Tiny steps to fill big shoes

Birthday cake, party balloons and lots of toys.

Hip, Hip, Hurray - Harry is one today.

Part 2:

First steps in the sand,
First steps on the land,
First steps left dangling,
First steps paddling,
First steps in the park,
First steps along the lane,
First steps across the meadow,
First steps in the rain,
First steps feeling pain,
First steps tiny and slow,
First steps tip – toe,
First steps feel sleepy,
First steps in the dark,
First steps under cover,
First steps, sleeping until tomorrow.

Part 3:

First steps come in all shapes and sizes,
Scrawling to walking to running,
First day at nursery, school, college,
First words to talking to chatting,
First best mates, to lifelong friends,
First date, first kiss, first broken heart,
First job, first wage packet and beyond,
First drink, first holiday on your own,
First day after yesterday, until tomorrow.

Part 4:

The first time that I saw you, my heart missed a beat,
The first time we touched, butterflies jumped around my body,

The first time we kissed, your lips tasted so sweet,
The first time I asked you, you said yes,
The first day of the rest of our lives, is the greatest of them all.

Part 5:

There are so many first steps in life.

Valentine Weekend

You will always be my valentine,
More than words can say
I will love you more and more,
Each passing day

As the sun…through the broken clouds,
Warms my face, body and soul
Your image I can see,
Your presence I can feel

Your body I can touch,
Your lips I can trust
My faith in you, a must,
As I continue to lust

You can see…what I can feel,
You know, that I know the spiel
You and I are for real,
A cuddle can always seal a deal

Twelve red roses just for you,
A walk in the park
A kiss in the dark,
A whisper…can start a spark

Distance not an issue,
Travelling to see you
Counting the moments,
I can feel you

Closer and closer,
As the clock ticks down
The hour is near,
Your image sparks a memory

We will talk and we will walk,
Winter in full swing
Food festival in full flow,
Many treats, beer tasting and wine

Whispering sweet nothing's,
Laughing out loud
Smiling all around,
Snowing on the ground

Dusting away, this special winter's day,
Counting the minutes, hours and days
We will meet again very soon,
Only 364 days to the next Valentine weekend.

(For Lisa)

The Kiss

It's the kiss that I should have taken,
The one not to be missed,
To this day, I wonder why I walked away?
Many years now and I still imagine the look in her eye.

Over the years many kisses have come and gone,
The friendly, the peck on the cheek, the blow in the air,
The innocent, the lost, the passionate,
The dying kiss.

Two sets of lips resting against each other,
Body heating up all over, turning cold into warmth,
All around invisible, to the mind and reality,
Giving away to an experience like no other.

I can still see and feel that missed kiss,
Those eyes and tender smile, part of a beautiful vision,
Everywhere that I turn, everywhere that I step,
Night and day forming part of my daily dreams.

Like a thousand-piece jigsaw, all the parts coming together,
Arms wrapped around tightly, as smiles light up with a glimmer of hope,
It's the kiss that I should have taken,
The one not to be missed.

The Connection (The Spark)

(for that special someone)

It all started with a text,
A few months after exchanging phone numbers,
A reply came through the digital airways,
Almost instantly.

Messages passed with the help of our thumbs,
Where we arranged a meet up,
The place to be a local café,
Seated at a table facing outwards across the square.

Early afternoon followed late morning,
In the blink of an eye it was time to say goodbye,
Timed passed all too quickly,
No awkward pauses resting between you & I.

Making chatting ever so easy from one person to another,
The spark between us was there for all to see,
The connection in the palm of our hands,
Parting was hard for one or maybe both, I don't really know.

As we moved in separate directions,
All I wanted to do was to turn around and kiss you,
I should have taken this opportunity to embrace you,
Now wishing that I had felt those beautiful lips.

Theme: Luck / plus using the word **'in it'**, at the end of each line, on the first poem only.

Note: The title for the first poem is taken from a Chinese fortune cookie, except the last word **'in-it'**, that was added by the class tutor.

'Old friends make the best friends' in it

Old friends make the best friends init,
But can old friends be true friends init,
Can your pet be an intelligent friend init?
Can social friends be best friends init,
Can group friends be your true friends init,
Can family friends be the real friend init?
Can social media friends be any kind of friend init?

....

A Poem

Good Luck, No Luck, Any Luck Will Do

Cats (waving or not) I have owned five and with very little luck
They say cats have nine lives, but my Flash, Elton and John, Two Toes and Sooty, after living with me, felt one was enough?

Even Snowy my rabbit hopped up to heaven, her left foot
I held in my hand as a symbol of hope and promise,
Lucky rabbits' foot as the old wise saying goes

Wishing that the next pet that I owned would live past one
& ¾

How I held that foot in my hand, ever so so tightly
Eyes closed and wishing hard, ever so hard,
Fingers crossed, toes crossed, in fact everything crossed

Wishing that the next pet that I owned would live past one
& ¾

Until my tortoise Samson sprinted off to a better land
They say pets come and go, mine just go, far far away,
Friends ask me to dog sit / walk Jaffa, Chase & Otis

With the most common question of all, hey Paddy
'Why is it not, that you don't have a pet of your own'?
As I am so good with all of their pets' needs

I look back at my friends, while fussing over their little treasures
I stand and stare, nodding in agreement, while scratching my bald head,
Smiling at this pleasant thought, before answering that I am always

Wishing that the next pet that I owned would live past one
& ¾

Super Saturday 2015 (Six Nations / Part 2)
(Refer to *In A Word* for part 1)

Super Saturday twenty fifteen,
Lived up to its name…in the name of the game,
Nine weekends, filled with fifteen battles,
Of fantastic, nail biting rugby

From the first end of winter, weekend in February,
Straight through to the last, start of spring weekend in March,
We had it all…missed penalties, solo tries,
Drop goals, collapsed rucks, red cards…

You name it, it all spilled out onto the battlefield,
Blood, sweat and the occasional knock to the head,
Tackles, there were many, sin bin for ten, down to fourteen men,
The boys came close, down in the Welsh capital

And just as we were all thinking,
That this competition couldn't get any better?
On the fourteenth day, of the third month,
In what seemed like a mild day, down in Cardiff

An unforeseen, thunderstorm would erupt,
Developing into the highlight of the tournament,
As the Irish…2014 retaining champions,
Up against the Welsh masters of the field

Produced an unbroken thirty-three passes,
But were unable to get past, a red wall blocking them,
One metre from the try line

Excitement at its highest, people on the edge of their seats,
You daren't take your eyes away from the action,

As missing a single moment, of the greatness match,
In the past seven years, would be a rugby 'fan' crime!!

Culminating into a Super Saturday,
Four weeks later, as the closest fought,
Six nations championship in years, delivered its final blow

First of all we had the Italian boys v the Welsh lions,
Followed by the Scots tartans v the Irish warriors,
Then to top the day off, the English rose v the French army,
No grand slam to be had, just points to be gained

Seven hours of nail-biting action,
As ninety supreme athletes, took this great tournament,
Down to the wire,
One minute…One metre…One try.

I Love Pubs

I've been to many pubs over the years, city pubs, country pubs,
Loud pubs, quiet pubs, spit & sawdust pubs,
Family pubs & not so friendly pubs…

I Love Pubs

But my favourite pub of all time, has to be the Barrels,
You can turn up on your own & never be alone,
Meet friends, writers, poets & musicians for a chat & a pint…
Or two, of Wye Valley's best brew…

I Love Pubs

A game of pool or three for only 50p & free on a Tuesday,
Quiet time for a read in the big, well-kept beer garden,
With free newspapers & magazines at your disposal…

I Love Pubs

Free music nights & fun to be had…when the Cider City Jazzmen,
Make their monthly appearance…

I Love Pubs

The Barrels, where everyone knows your name,
Pop up food tents for the big sporting events,
Carryout's & fresh farm eggs by the dozen…

I Love Pubs

The highlight of the week, Sunday lunchtime roast spuds & sausages…
What a little treat,

Followed by the highlight of the year, the four – day beer / music festival…
That raises thousands for charity…

I Love Pubs

My personal favourite, a happy hour that lasts for 120 minutes…

I Love the Barrels.

One Pint of Dark, One Pint of Black and One Pint of Stout

(For my Welsh friend Steven)

Facing Principality Rugby Stadium, Cardiff,
Steven & I find ourselves at the City Arms public house,
A harmonica accompanying the music coming from afar,
What's you're poison my friend asks me, from the handsome display?

**But all I really want is,
One pint of dark, one pint of black and one pint of stout**

As the melody of Bob Dylan shouts out from the 'open mic',
The singer, song writing guitar player continues doing his thing,
International beers and lager of the finest quality on display,
Even a menu to help the customer choose.

**But all I really want is,
One pint of dark, one pint of black and one pint of stout**

You can have this one or you can have that one,
Beers from Belgium, France, Canada and further afield,
My friend explains to me, as we discuss,
Brexit, rugby and the state of the economy.

But all I really want is,
One pint of dark, one pint of black and one pint of stout

Twenty thousand people had gathered on Barry Island,
On New Year's Day, I inform my friend,
Australian, American, South African you can have the lot,
It's like Pandora's box, pleads my mate.

But all I really want is,
One pint of dark, one pint of black and one pint of stout

Look, let me show you the menu,
OK, let me have a look I respond,
You'll be impressed my friend,
Steven says with desperation creeping into his voice.

But all I really want is,
One pint of dark, one pint of black and one pint of stout

I give up my friend says in despair,
I'm sorry I say to my friend,
It's OK my friends replies,
I continue to explain.

But all I really want is,
One pint of dark, one pint of black and one pint of stout

Bloody English he says, bloody Welsh I reply,
Now what! my friend asks?
I suppose one of us should get the drinks in I say,

It's your round Steven says, with that lovely Welsh smile of his.

But all I really want is,
One pint of dark, one pint of black and one pint of stout

What's your fancy I ask my friend?
I don't really know he replies,
Well look at the menu I say,
I think I'll have what you're having he responds.

But all I really want is,
One pint of dark, one pint of black and one pint of stout

Dazzo the Dazzler

(Inspired by True Events)

It was the middle of the festive week,
The year twenty sixteen coming to an end,
Happy hour, happy for some,
People gathered in good cheer, with lots of beer.

Friends and family milling around,
Cheers, cheers to you all,
Glad tidings just around the corner,
Mine's a pint, what's yours?

Bike parked upright and chained to the railings,
Money in hand, as the main man enters the grounds,
Striding down the cobbled beer garden,
The crowds parting as he swaggers forward.

Heads turning here and there,
Nodding in acknowledgement,
At this ruffled guy we all know,
As the Dazzler enters the arena.

Fifty pence all the money he will need,
Owning the pool table for the evening,
With his smooth arm action and the
Magic cue clenched in both hands.

A dazzling display is brought to life,
As the frames rack up and where no one is taken prisoner,
Trick shots galore; miss at your peril,
Not one, not two, not three or even four.

Seven nil will be the final score,

As we all sit and wonder, where our friend gets his talent,
He just struts his stuff and smiles shyly,
Giving the years-old answer, it's just the luck of the draw.

Mince pies and mistletoe,
Candles and Christmas decorations,
Snow on its way, a frost all around,
As the man we know as the Dazzler rides into the night.

The Pleasure of Smoking

Introduction

I was brought up with a father who smoked cigarettes while working, a pipe while relaxing and cigars for those special occasions.

A grandmother who smoked Park Drive, no filter and full tarred. None of this blue packet, filter cobblers!

My grandmother also liked to sniff snuff; I've never really understood the purpose of snuff. But there you go everyone to their own.

I have been to a few parties and festivals in my time, where all sorts were smoked. However, I hasten to add, not for me.

I have also been a cigarette smoker, back in my youth. But what I really enjoy now is a nice cigar. I have a small collection of cigars at home that have been given to me as gifts and I hope that one day that I will enjoy them for their main purpose.

On a day-to-day basis I smoke mini cigars, mainly Hamlets, but I do like a variety and normally with a pint of stout at my local, the Barrels.

What I am going to try and do with this poem is give my personal account of the pleasure of smoking.

....

The Pleasure of Smoking / Part 1

Childhood memories are made of many things,
Trips to the park with your grandparents,
Mother's Sunday roast with all the trimmings,
Receiving a pat on the back from dad for a special achievement.

Visits to uncle's and auntie's homes, playing with cousins,
Both in your own country and abroad,
Family holidays, school holidays, bank holidays,
Having school friends stay for sleep over.

School trips away from parents,
Weekends staying at grandparents,
Believing in Father Christmas,
Easter egg treasure hunts.

And so on...

However, my childhood memories are made from,

Smoking, beer, whisky and cards,

Dad working in the garden, with smoke billowing from his mouth,
Relaxing in the evening with his pipe, pipe tobacco and all the tools,
That accompanies this hobby,

Cigars held back for special occasions, anniversaries, special birthdays,
Christenings, weddings, and funerals,

As an adult I have only come across one other person who smokes a pipe,
A colleague and when he used to light up, the smell of the smoke would remind me,
Of those evenings at home, when I was a child.

....

The Pleasure of Smoking / Part 2

The tin of snuff lay on the side of the table,

Next to the twenty pack of Park Drive,

Nan was shuffling the playing cards,

With a ciggy hanging from her mouth,

Pass me the whisky Paddy…pass me the whisky,

My pocket money and her pension lay between us,

Dixie lay beneath the table,

The stakes were high and I was allowed to stay up late,

As there was no school the next day.

....

The Pleasure of Smoking / Part 3

Myself, I like to enjoy a smoke with a pint of beer, mainly stout,

After work, on an evening out, when you open your cigar box &

Select the one to light up, with the red flame helping as you inhale,

The relief as you blow out smoke, relax, distress, and unwind,

Tap the ashtray; take a sip from your beer, enjoy your own company,

Read the daily newspaper and chat to the locals, put the world to right,

It's happy hour and only two pounds for a pint of beer,

Cigars come in all shapes and sizes,

Be careful how you select, as these days they come in blue low tar packs,

And some even filtered, bloody double filtered in fact!

Sirens

(Inspired by Moving Back into the City)

On the edge of town, down the fast lane

Sirens come and sirens go

Very near, almost on top of you

Yet so far away…it could take all day

In the distance you can hear them pass,

They are very fast.

Very fast or almost slow,

Ignoring green and amber…through red they go

Don't stand too close…

No time to finish a brew…as you recover from the overdose.

Sirens all sound different,

Police, ambulances and the fire drivers too…

Air ambulance is a special one…for the hikers with no sense.

Sirens racing very fast, you might miss them if you blink

Accidents come in all shapes and sizes,

To make us all sit up and think.

Sirens helping everyone on the brink

Keeping us all wise, so that we don't sink.

Sirens just like the wind...comes so fast,

It could almost make one spin...

Always fasten your seatbelts.

As sirens race for everyone...no matter who we are

So that none of us...

Will ever have to contact our next of kin.

One Day Summer Holiday

As I put my old round sunglasses back on,
Shades of sky blue come to view,
A style that was so cool back in the day.

Nineteen thirty that was the year

As I sit with the sun shining above me,
I'm going to relax in my favourite chair,
To while away a few hours.

As a nap can make you seem brand new

It's amazing what you can feel,
Is it a dream or a memory?
It's tea and biscuits now I'm retired.

No more beer and fags for me

When I close my eyes everything seems so near,
As I'm at one with my family,
And on the day that we travelled to the coast.

After the factory closed its large iron gates.

This was a very good time for us all as a fold,
With the shade covering my eyes,
I can feel the sea breeze and laughter on the wind.

As the children unpacked the special treats

Cockles, prawns, mussels, whelks,
Candyfloss, toffee apples,
Delicious ice cream and lots of sweets.

Washed down with homemade lemonade

With time to waste just for this one day,
Into the water they encouraged us,
So with our skirt and trouser legs pulled up high.

We could feel the sand between our toes

The cold of the waves catching us by surprise,
As the grime of the factory washed away into the sea,
The reality being that this was our escapism.

When I took my family on our one-day summer holiday

The Four Seasons

Spring / Summer / Autumn / Winter

Spring

Spring sunshine, anew as the last winter frosts melt away,
Morning dew hanging from the barbecue,
The vegetable patch untouched, fallen pears from above,
Soil running along an unkempt lawn.

As I step down onto my patio, entering a new world,
The pyracantha comes into sight, bringing new light,
Amongst the bed of scattered leaves, many colours fade away,
Cold, silent and soft this new world may seem.

As winter becomes a memory and a new season enters our land,
A breeze blows away the cobwebs, as the dark nights turn so bright,
Unwrap the garden furniture, unlock the shed, winter has gone to bed,
Sweep away the dust, as yellow sunshine, so bright, is a delight.

Summer

Warm sunshine, summer glow, mown grass and taking it slow,
Salads and fish for tea, cool lemonade with ice, very nice,
Evening walks along the river, an ice cream or two,
Only a beer garden will do, for you and me.

Children playing as the sunshine comes out for a day,
Family picnics, summer holidays down by the sea,
Young couples courting and walking along the riverside,
As fishermen and canoeists take in the view.

As I take a sip from my tea, I watch next door's cat,
Crawl along my garden wall, hunting she may be,
Coming from miles around to feed, are the sweet sight and sound,
A tree Sparrow, Blackbird, Red Wing and a Robin just to name a few.

The barbecue alive with lots of fire,
Piles of meat wait by the side, buttered rolls and lots of sauces,
Friends and family gather with lots of beer and laughter,
Dry days; turn into long bright and light open nights.

Autumn

As the daylight fades slowly away, a few minutes each day,
A rainbow of colours blossom from the trees,
Yellow, orange and green can be seen,
As leaves fall to the ground making little sound.

Crunchy under foot, as the sound of autumn can be heard,
Woolly hats, scarves and gloves seem far away,
As clouds circle overhead, giving way to so many beautiful colours,
Brown, red, orange, yellow and blue reappear as new.

As I stand on my patio, a winter day hangs in the air,
Skies mixed with so many stories,
I wonder when I will hear the thunder,
Lightning strikes from high above, all around.

Winter

Short days / long days and very many dark nights,
As daylight comes into view slowly,
Leaving us as fast as it came,
Darkness all around us from morning to dusk.

Full power and red alert, all before a morning cup of tea,
Open fires, electric blankets, hats and scarves,
Keeping the warm within and Mr Frost at bay,
Dark, cold and wet, not my favourite ingredients.

Open black skies, full of stars, glittering above,
Red being the warning, that a new day is dawning,
Wind, rain, frost and snow, all on a go-slow,
The shortest day, followed by the longest night.

Everything slowing down, falling under that winter spell,
As I hold my hot drink with both hands,
It's only mid-afternoon, as I glance at my plants,
The daylight fading.

All is quiet and peaceful.

A tercets / poem

River Carnival (2016)

Friday night is launch night
Light the touch and set it right
So that we can all see the light

The rain has eased,
You will be pleased,
However, there is still a cool breeze

As crowds gather along the river Wye,
Clouds clear giving way to an open sky,
It's simple you see and I can simplify

Dancers on stage performing,
As the audience continue forming,
The whole experience is storming

As we stand and we cheer,
It becomes clear,
I can see something in the water appear

Lanterns moving along in the dark,
Fluorescent jackets bring a certain spark,
As the sun settles and night grows darker

Candle lights beautify,
As the ripples electrify,
Glow in the dark butterfly

Fireworks set the dark sky alight,
Everywhere around is bright,
The perfect end to a beautiful night.

The Day I Met Benjamin

It was a hot July summer's day as I stepped onto the 476 bus,
Travelling through the beautiful Herefordshire countryside,
The international Ledbury Poetry Festival was in my sight.

Just a stone's throw from the Malvern Hills,
Lies this small black and white market town,
That once a year comes into its own,
As poets from the globe come to sample the quiet life.

These giants from the literary world,
Leave their comfort zones of the big city lights,
London, Belfast and New York just to name a few,
They find themselves down in the valleys.

Shopkeepers greeting regulars by their first name,
While the bakery, greengrocer, cobbler, and teashops,
Welcome new and old into their fold.

And as the town crier mingles with the crowds, spreading the news.

There was just one man that I was here to see,
A Birmingham boy just like me,
He goes by the name of Benjamin you see.

A beat poet with some attitude…writing with a political view.

Market house to community hall,
Was the route that I had to take,
On arrival at my destination,
The sign read Mr Zephaniah has sold out.

Families before me were starting to take the best seats,
As I moved slowly along the middle and found a good spot,
Taking my place amongst the excited audience,
Only five rows separated centre stage and me.

A Master of Performance poetry and a pure delight,
Performing for adults and children alike,
Stage presence and honesty in his chosen words,
Covering global issues, social justice and much, much more.

But the highlight of my day came right at the end,
As not only did Benjamin autograph his new book,
He also posed for a photograph alongside me,
One for the album, wouldn't you agree?

A Matter of Honour

He
Raised
His
Father's
Pistol
The
Family
Heirloom
His
Hand
Was
Shaking
As
He
Had
Never
Fired
A
Gun
Before

He
Had
Challenged
The
Other
Gentleman
To
A
Duel
For
Insulting
His
Wife

Aim
High
Aim
Low
As
Straight
As
An
Arrow
With
Anger
Running
Through
His
Veins

Take
Your
Pistols
To
Draw

His
Was
So
Big
A
Shining
Example
Of
Riviere
Craftsmanship
A
Gun
Maker's

Finest

Hers
So
Small
And
Almost
Naked
To
The
Eye

He   Tried
Very   Very
Hard   To

                        Miss

Thunderstone

'Be careful of the falling rocks!'
As a flurry of stones, fall to the ground,
Bouncing onto the footpath & into the sea,
Nestling far below, resting on the seabed

A whistling wind, taking control,
Different sounds can be heard,
Conductor in place, as the orchestra warms up,
Director's final call / Ready to raise the roof

A show in progress, the sound of rumbling from far below,
On a dark winter's night, walking along the sea front,
Listening to the music of the wild,
The opera, the ushers, the audience taking their seats

The calm before the main event,
Screaming / heavy rain, bringing a mixture of sounds,
Music stirring in the distance,
Mighty waves starting to make an impact

The ambience on standby,
Musicians ready to take control,
Deep, deep in the chorus pit below,
Movement that seems far, far away

Clocks going back, an hour extra sleep,
The end of summer, short days and long dark nights,
Fireworks on display, lighting up the sky,
Bonfire night only a few hours away

Steady for a thousand years –
The giant striding along the sandy beach,
The rope bridge too weak, to carry the mighty weight,

Sea / Water filling the big holes left by massive feet

A thousand light bulbs, gliding over the ocean,
A dark stillness, that goes on forever,
The hero getting ready for the final curtain call,
The storm ready to show

Coming Home

Leaving the main train station behind and
Finding myself on Commercial Road,
It's the smell of the KFC you see,
Staying with me while heading for high town.

Negotiating my way through market day, while
Passing through Church Street with its cobbled footpaths,
Where lies The Lichfield Vaults Inn streaming with history?
Enjoy fine ales, stout, and daily lunch time specials.

Live rock and blues on a Sunday afternoon

The Cathedral coming into my view,
Where Herefordions welcomes old and new,
As I take my seat in the Chapter house gardens.
The Friday afternoon jazz session is in full flow.

Summer has arrived as young and old enjoy free live music,
Homemade cakes, earl grey tea, salads and desserts to lust after,
Bulmer's cider and Wye Valley's ale are just a few of the items for you,
To enjoy if you're feeling naughty, just like me.

Swing, jazz, Latin, folk, what's your passion, they deliver it all

Crossing the Left Bank Bridge and walking along the river Wye,
Fishermen wait and pray for the catch of the day,
Children playing on the fields, cycle routes in full display,
Joggers moving fast each way.

On to castle green, dog walkers strolling along in their own thoughts,
A bowls game is in full swing, toddlers feeding the ducks,
Couples, families, young and old chatting, laughing, playing on the grass,
While the ice cream man is selling out fast through this mini heat wave.

No rush as it's a warm and sunny cloudless day

Shops, pubs and cafes trading with customers before me,
While making my way along the busy Gaol Street,
Settling in the main square, market day still in full swing,
I sit outside the black and white house, facing the big black bull.

In the distance I can see the Royal National College for the Blind,
Sitting at the top of Aylestone Hill, just a short walk from the Hereford / Ludlow, not forgetting the Art / Design College,
All joined together like a Rosary bead.
Just to add, the beautiful Hereford Cathedral as night-time falls, is a welcome sight

Sitting in the Barrels pool room,
Sipping a pint of stout or two,
This is a welcome rest and a
Sure sign that I am finally home.

Too Soon

It all seems too soon
Leaves falling all around &
Crackling under foot
Walking paths hidden,

Around the Cathedral green
As a glimmer of hope comes
Breaking through
With a rainbow of colours,

We hope that winter
Doesn't come too soon
Dark by eight
It will soon be Christmas,

But it's only mid-September
As the clouds gather above
Collar up on my winter coat
As I stroll down Church Street,

Crossing into high town
Farmers' market in full flow
Open plan coffee shops
Serving steaming hot drinks,

The sky grows darker
As I step under cover
And order a brew
One, two, three,

Brollies pop open,
As people move faster,
Shelter becoming a safe place
Where everyone wants to be,

Wind getting stronger
As hailstones come crashing down
Puddles everywhere you step
Only one thing to do,

And

That's to order another brew.

The following work is inspired by the Art Exhibition, held at Hereford Library.
'I am not who you think I am' by Heather Bowring

Touch and Feel What is Real?

1:

The voices all around me tell me that I have arrived,
The shuddering lift tells me, that I do not have to climb the creaky stairs,

My guide dog tells me that this is a safe place for me to be.

The library assistant tells me that the art exhibition is free to attend,

My guide dog tells me that I have reached my final destination,

The museum assistant tells me that there are no dogs allowed.

I tell my guide dog to sit and wait patiently for my return,

The museum assistant tells me that I can feel, touch and hear the artwork on display,

I tell everyone, I am not who you think I am.

One Thousand and Out

(Sonnet)

2:

The year, nineteen hundred and thirty nine,
I was a young girl, heading to what fate?
Volunteering to fight on the front line,
Defending our land, beyond the pearly gate.

I will never dream, as once before,
World war two, innocent souls, if only you knew,
It felt like a hundred years, not just four,
Settling in, with my very special crew.

Fighting high above, through heaven and hell,
Dozens of missions, I flew, fought and survived,
Those of us who marched on, who could tell,
We're the lucky ones, to still be alive.

My life, may never recover from war,
Climbing one thousand skies, counting…no more.

Brothers in Arms

We came into the world, only fifteen months apart,
Pure white, with a little pink thrown in, the colour of life

Brothers in arms for seventeen years,
Before the life of the rainbow faded from our lives,
Yellow, red, orange, blue and violet...

At first everything seemed to be black and white,
Through our glittering tears, as darkness fell over us,
Before the colour of life was taken away,
The greyness of conflict, the colour of death

Many shades of red...flowing like rivers,
Dusty smoke, covering the sight of the
Yellowing bodies that lay before us,
The rainbow fading before our very eyes,
Dark / black clouds covering the land

Seventeen years before our lives changed forever,
Seventeen years before the bright light turned to darkness,
Seventeen years before the old bearded man
Took us up, towards the white fluffy clouds in the sky,
As we look over our free, green and pleasant land,
Brothers in arms joined by two medals...forever.

Street Underground Performance

Act 1:

A warm bright sunshine falling across my face,
As I walk along, taking the breeze in my stride,
Mixing in with the morning rush…rush hour if I must,
Human traffic caught up together, in an ongoing fight.

No time to stand still, think and stare,
An elbow or two for good measure, if I dare,
As I guide myself around screaming school kids,
And old ladies with trolleys on wheels.

Dodging a cyclist, motor-scooters, and pushchairs,
Heading down the ramp, two-way blank expressions,
Daydreaming…all just wanting to go back to bed,
The walking dead, robots…too much going on in our heads.

Dogs held on leads, at many lengths ahead of their masters,
Be careful not to fall, trip or stall…keep close to the wall,
A pickpocket or two, maybe out to get you, the chance we all take,
Excuse me sir…can you show the way, to any spare change?

Trying very hard not to think about, what's on the other side,
Adults and children, heading out to the working world,
The dark, cold, damp underpass calling us all,
To escape this deafening noise all around, for a few quiet moments.

On the tarmac and concrete high above,
Horns blowing, sirens racing…as the trapped,

Take a sneaky glance towards a hidden world…
A dark…forgotten…underground world…just out of reach.

Footpaths heaving and roads full to the hilt,
Bodies everywhere, young, mature and aged,
The empty space, the empty stare, on an empty stage,
Too busy to slow down…smile or even care.

Descending down into the hidden world of darkness,
As I enter the world below, the first things to hit me,
Aren't the litter, nicotine butts, cider cans and broken bottles!!
It's the dark, damp, cold, and urine smelling graffiti filled walls.

The surreal attempt at someone, creating a makeshift home,
Cardboard city, the begging, busking, music and so-called art,
The loyal mutt, sat beside the old rusty battered soup tin,
Where we all feel obliged, to drop our loose shrapnel.

Actors we all tend to be…life the great performance,
For only the strong, mighty, and well rehearsed…
The great script, spelt, thrown and spread out in front of us,
The cast versus the audience…whom are we to judge?

Act 2:

As the clocks go back, winter starts its slow attack,
Dark in the morning, in the afternoon, and on the way home,
Sleet, snow, ice and lots of cold damp weather,
Be careful where you walk, black ice under foot.

The underpass suddenly comes in our sight,

With a trickling of poor grey light, black and white…
Rain 'like' drops, fall all around us from the ceiling just above,
A tingle of happiness starts to grip us, or could this be fear?

As we, you and I decide on taking the ramp,
Lots of pushchairs, pushbikes and wheelchairs…
Re-appear in our way…steps it's easy to say,
As the hidden underground world pulls us all, ever nearer.

Leaving the dark, loud, busy world high above,
Pimps, hookers, beggars and tramps too,
The scent of stale alcohol, hanging in the air,
Too far beaten, they sleep where they choose to droop.

As I hurry to reach the end of the dark grey tunnel,
A few hours ago, I wouldn't have felt this way,
I see the end of the light…the end in my sight,
With a great urge to make it home tonight.

I need the loo, a strip of urine…
Melting down the graffiti filled walls,
Bubblegum, chewing tobacco, a roll up nearing its life,
Dropping the nub end, that dissolves out of sight.

Is it a performance…or is it real?
Real life performance at a steal,
The great show of life…the stage we all perform on,
Is it really made up of heroes and villains?

Today's performance nearing the final curtain.

Act 3:

As winter fades and the clocks go forward,
An hour less sleep, is not a lot to ask,

For some extra daylight and less fear,
As the hidden world appears in our sight.

Light and bright in the early morning rush,
Polite smiles and interactions re-appear,
Eyes hiding behind dark shades,
Shadows, following us through the two-way tunnel.

The sharpness from the street above,
Falling / flowing down into the underground,
Flexing all around, different sides are razor sharp,
As the day moves forward and out of sight.

Cardboard city, slowly disappearing,
Un-washed bedding, lying in its wake,
The homeless, the tramps, the fallen,
Pleading / begging and simply asking for a penny or two.

They sit and they stare, the sunshine warming their fragile bodies,
Tatty hat in hand, on the edge of the city, the edge of life,
Our clean smiles look down from behind our dark shades,
As we drop our loose change in the filthy / battered cloth.

As the sad, dirty, un-kept and dare I say, un-loved,
Shell of a person, looks up, squinting from the bright light,
A yellow smile, with words that are so shallow,
We both dismiss them with our pitying stares.

Keep moving, head upright, out of sight, out of mind,
I'm suddenly on my corner, home time in my view,
Smiling from the inside, as I move closer to comfort,
Locking my front door behind me, locking out this mad world.

I take my bow and bid you all good night.

Theme: Magna Carta / Exhibition (1215-2015)

The Story Of The Song

The story of the song continues its long journey.

The story of the song,
Lyrics that have lasted eight hundred years,
The choir…the soft voices,
Music continues to travel.

The story of the song,
The voice, the music and the lyrics,
Screaming and shouting to be heard,
Crying many tears over the years.

The story of the song,
Began its journey in black and white,
Travelling through decades,
War…after bloody war.

The story of the song,
Has a tainted past,
Red tempers, cause fighting,
Waves splash against the grey rocks.

The story of the song,
Eight hundred years of spilling blood,
Fighting honour and many battles,
A mighty long time, to hope for peace.

The story of the song,
Promised peace and freedom,

The icon of justice for all,
Words that meant something, once.

The story of the song,
Written by well meaning hands,
Abused and used by others,
Broken words...broken promises.

The story of the song,
Keeping alive the changing scenery of our land,
Where the castle once stood still,
Dominating our great city.

The story of the song,
Staying alive, through the cathedral walls,
Music never standing still,
A melody for all ages.

The story of the song,
Strong words, strong laws, strong views,
Written in concrete, with a mighty strong pen,
Where men once ruled and women once, obeyed.

The story of the song,
Who knew, how long these views would last,
Leaving the past behind, looking to the future,
Bringing the new world into Technicolour.

The story of the song still has a long journey ahead.

Gravy Rap (No More Gravy)

(Inspired by a Broken Antique Plate)

The throwaway society,
Has no time to make real gravy,
As the staple gun has no more worth,
Boil some water, as granules will do.

Buried in history are the gunmen of staple past

As the staple guns lay by the roadside,
Modern age has taken over the gravy train,
As when our appliances give up the plight,
We simply throw them away.

No more real stock, to flavour our meat and two veg

Broken plates are simply binned,
As a sticky paste has replaced the staples
that were once drawn,
And the throwaway society is here to stay.

No more quick fix for the families of the gunmen

One hundred and sixty-three years, since passed,
As the last staple attached itself
to the bottom of the antique plate,
Slowing the drip…drop…drip…drop…

Of modern society…the throwaway society

Taking all the leftovers from the rubbish bin
and mixing the entire ingredients,

Producing super-fast...super glue.

That has replaced the soul of the staple man

A quick fix for me and you,
Saving gravy plates from the trash,
That was once brought back to life?

By the faithful staple gunman and his wife

Grand Ma Mooney's Irish Coddle

As we prepare to lose an hour's sleep,
And the dark nights creep up on us,
With the cold winter falling all around us.

This gets me thinking of days gone by,
When my Grand Ma Mooney,
Would make her famous three-day stew.

As I head to the Saturday market in high town,
Most of my ingredients can be bought from,
Pete's organic vegetable market stall.

Leeks, potatoes, carrots, swede, parsnips
And only white onions, as red will not do.
Sausage and bacon to add to the pot,
Lentils from the corner shop.

Dumplings prepared and added
To the casserole dish,
Just before I cover with gravy (not to thick).

Fresh crusty bread with lashings of butter,
Wait by the side, as the final twist,
In preparation to this delicious meal.

Placing everything into the warm oven,
I find myself with an hour to spare,

So along with a steaming strong cup of tea
and my childhood memories for company.

I sit patiently waiting with anticipation,
Looking forward to enjoying,
My Grand Ma Mooney's three day coddle.

The only way to end a long winter's day

Blanket

Seventeen days, two weeks & thirty-six hours earlier,
The blanket had returned, darkness taking control,
Covering my body from head to toe.

A dark cloud hovering above,
Sunshine & light fading out of sight,
Loneliness creeping in,
Hope fading away.

Feeling lonely & out of the loop,
As friends & family stay quiet,
Not knowing what to do or what to say.

Sharing is the only way forward,
Letting others know,
Talking / speaking / explaining can be hard,
Almost impossible.

Finding the strength to remove the blanket,
To undo the knots, unfasten the cord,
Breathe my friend…breathe.

There is strength in lifting the darkness.
Letting a glimmer of light in,
I know this can be hard,
But you can do this my friend.

Find that inner strength & fight that darkness,

Reach out to someone,
By speech, by phone, by text, by email.

Seventeen days, two weeks & thirty-seven hours,
The dark cloud is lifting,
A burst of energy is returning,
The blanket is loosening its grip.

Someone is listening,
Reach out & someone will be there.
I am here my friend, with you and for you.

Invisible Body & Lost Soul

As I continued staring, a ghost greeted me from the glass reflection on the wall,
Who is this person looking back at me?
A shadow of someone I once knew.

You see, it was the dose that I had pulled into the needle, a thousand times before.

Measuring, the right amount, had become an art form,
The easy way to say,
The only way to say.

Helping me through the long grey days, weeks, months, years and many fears.

One, two, three and four…before relief comes knocking on the door,
Sitting upright, on the wooden floor,
Arm flexed and muscles tightened…don't be frightened.

Long, strong leather belt, wrapped so tight…I feel no shame.

Placing the syringe close to my skin, calculating the exact moment of impact,
Weighing up the odds of relief and dare,
Does anyone care?

Fist clinched, teeth pulling down, on a taste of pure peace.
Body and soul focused.

Sweat pouring, heart racing…clock ticking so loud, I almost cry,

The weight on my shoulders so heavy,
A ton to one, if I live or die?

Four, three, two, one, thumb pressing down, as needle empties in the blink of an eye.

Who is that shell of a person, looking into my lost reflection,
Looking out onto a cloud of dust,
Sleeping forever…no more lies.

As high as a kite…Tears falling, like raindrops from the lord above.

You see, I over did the amount, by a fraction of a point,
The art form broken like a shell,
A thousand times and one…not to be taken lightly / or not to be done at all.

Ghost Train

Scanner reads 'train running late',
Loud voice on overhead speakers
Shout 'delayed train arriving in five',
Yellow line reads 'do not cross'.

On this dark and cold winter's night,
Stars shine above me as I climb the steps,
To board the train, homeward bound.

Wandering along the empty carriages,
I feel the stares passing through me,
Heads upright, eyes locked straight ahead,
Shallow silhouettes bouncing back from the reflection.

Shadows come and settle all around me,
As I reach the end of the isle and take my seat,
Waiting for the ticket man.

In whom do we trust?

On reaching my destination,
White words shout, 'trains stop here',
Yellow line highlights 'do not cross'.

Crossing over the bridge to my exit,
I continue to step from the station,
Where taxis are waiting for a fare,
They will drive me if they-there.

As I walk towards home,
A railing divides me from the tracks,
As the empty carriages stand idling away.

I stand and stare, as a whistle blows,
I stand and stare, but can see no one there,
As the train moves from the tracks,
Is this real or just a dream?

When I open my eyes,
I reach across and rest my hand,
Upon my ticket' stubs.

Looking on from the Outside

Looking on from the outside

Welcome, welcome, welcome,
Being greeted by friends, handshakes & kisses,
Hugs…saying that I have missed you,
Acknowledgements, from across the room.

The wave of a hand, the nod of a head, the blink of an eye,
Everyone gathered at the Coach House,
The left bank side of the river Wye,
'That will be seven pounds please' with your stamp of a butterfly.

Musicians setting up, guitars, banjoes, harmonica on display,
Everyone idly chatting, warm welcomes are here to stay,
Beer, cider and wine, glasses clinking, cheers, cheers, cheers,
The round stairs leading to the bar, up & down, up & down.

Looking on from the outside

Tablecloths pressed, glasses polished, beer mats in place,
Candles on display, lighting up the tables,
Just like on Christmas day, the atmosphere festive,
Xmas eve only four weeks away, too give & receive.

Black Friday will be a memory, bargains galore,
Santa and his sleigh delivering lots of presents,
Enjoying a mince pie, & a glass of sherry,
Not forgetting a carrot for the red nosed reindeer.

The first band in full flow, followed by the second & the third,

Soft voices, moving lips, with words, that bring the melody to life,
Every instrument doing its bit, with clapping from the audience,
All of us showing our appreciation.

Looking on from the outside,

Live music, folk music, honest songs,
Written from the heart & soul,
Real life stories, with a backing soundtrack,
Sad / laughing / smiling faces all around.

Stories with a twist, told through monologues,
Poetry…words joined together, like a giant jigsaw,
A story of love, a story of fate, a story of death,
The story of a wolf, with howling from dedicated fans.
As we all leave the Left Bank / Coach House,
By the open fire, with the open sky, falling stars,
Running alongside a big open river Wye,
Good nights, goodbyes, take care and see you soon.

Looking on from the outside.

Ballad

The Cowboy Within The Boy

It was over forty years ago now,
I was just a wee little blue-eyed boy,
When two action men heroes and their mares,
Came riding into my one-horse town.

Trigger a beautiful white Philly,
Bullet's tail wagging excitedly
& barking by his side,
Escaping into a fantasy far, far away.

Leaving my childhood world behind,
Putting my hat and gun belt on,
And becoming a cowboy for the day,
I was darn ready to fight the Wild West.

Setting the scene, igloos, campfires & fried beans,
Adventures would put us through the test,
Mounting our horses, me and my deputies,
Would show no fear, riding towards the unknown?

The heat like a melting pot, red dust blowing like a storm,
Mountains all around the Arizona desert,
The days were long, with the nights cool and short,
Clearly seeing the light, we were ready for the fight.

There be trouble, every town we went, with gambling,
Salons, whisky galore and chorus girls showing their corsets,
Robberies we would solve, gun fights we would win,
Gold mines would fall into our laps, as we lead our horses.

A thousand stars above the open candle lit sky,
Campfire and black coffee keeping us warm,

A banjo, harmonica & a song, idling our evenings away,
The dust would settle, the fire would fizzle down.

The Lone Ranger and Tonto tucked up in their camp beds,
Trigger with a blanket to keep him cosy and warm,
Bullet sleeping in his basket, a bowl of water by his side,
As I return home from my adventures, how real they feel.

Sausage, chips and beans for tea, a cowboy needs his strength,
Gun holster hanging on the back of my bedroom door,
My cowboy hat and marshal's badge sat on the side by my head,
As sleep looms over my body, dreams help my adventures continue.

Inspired by the Robert Gore Exhibition / Diary Of An Ordinary Criminal

Hereford Library (18th Jan - 5th Mar 2014)

Prisoner in Cell Rule 42 / SW21

No More Fear

1:

I want to die, to relieve the fear,
The guards believed the rumours,
They tell me not to hope,
Not to scream and not to dream.
My life is over, it may seem,
Breaking rule 42 is all I'm good for,
A wasted life, in a living shell.
Long dark days, locked up in silence,
As I wipe away the tears,
No more dope, to take the pain away.
Only one hour's exercise a day,
To stretch the mind and rewind,
I want to die, to relieve the fear.

Home Leave – Memories of Mid Wales / GL78

One Day

2:

One day they say,
One day to do with as I wish,
One day not to idle away,
One day not to worry and fear,

One day to slip out into the open air,
One day to embrace life for real,
One day to bring my dreams alive,
One day to see the mountains,
One day to feel the breeze,
One day to have a beer,
One day to open my eyes,
One day to feel like a human being,
One day they say.

Prisoner in Cell Rule 42 / SW21

Solitude

3:

Solitude, twenty-three taken from twenty-four,
From when they turn the key,
Emptiness falls all around.
Grub given through the little slit in the door,
Everything metal is the only sound you can hear,
Solitude, twenty-three taken from twenty-four.
My thoughts are my only company,
Except for the large mouse by the door.
As I protect myself from the blankness,
My mind races ahead…
Stopping, Stopping, Stopping, No More,
Solitude, twenty-three taken from twenty-four.

Home Leave – Memories of Mid Wales / GL78

Special Day

4:

Home leave is a special day,
As I wipe away the cobwebs,
Polish my shoes and dust down my best suit.
Descending from the prison steps,
My tummy starts to flutter,
A free man taking in the fresh air.
We catch each other's eyes, as I cross the road,
Its only when we kiss, I realise that this is not a dream.
Relaxing in the comfort of the convertible, we move at speed,
Leaving motorways, service stations and England behind,
Mid Wales is our final destination.
Mountains, waves so high, sand between our toes, picnic for two,
Home leave is a special day.

Prisoner in Cell Rule 42 / SW21

Emptiness

5:

Emptiness fills my wasted life,
Stuck between these four walls,
Left with only my regrets,

In despair, with no one to care.
I can't sink any lower,
As there is nowhere else to fall.
The cold concrete floor is where I land,
With only my slim body to keep me warm.
Thoughts turn into dreams,
Dreams turn into nightmares,
Hope turns into dust.
Rusting away in this dirty cell,
Emptiness fills my wasted Life.

Prisoner in Cell Rule 42 / SW21

Regret

6:

Regret is my punishment,
I ask 'is it too late?'
All alone in the dark,
No one to talk too, no more spark.
They tell me it's far too late,
As I'm a lost cause.
Rule 42 is never to be broken,
As the circumstances,
Will come knocking on your door.
Tired, cold and hungry,
All alone in my living hell.
My soul lost long ago,
Regret is my punishment.

A 'Reflection'

Super Sat 2019 / Six Nations - Part 3 (year of the comebacks)

Friday night, 1st February through to super Saturday, 16th March,

Seven weeks off blood…passion…tears and unbelievable drama,

Teams down and out…rising from the ashes…

France 16/0 ahead at half time against the mighty Welsh, who could foresee…

The fire roaring from the dragon, ending in a 25/20 win for the boys in red on French soil.

The first of not one…but two history-making comebacks…

We would have to wait for an agonising seven weeks to witness the thrashing of the green jersey warriors…delivered by the red dragons, on the eve of St-Patrick's day…No luck of the Irish that weekend!

Taking us up to the last game of the tournament for the Scots to show us all, that they are a force to be reckoned with… 31/0 down, five minutes from half time, before laying down their first of six tries…

Staging a remarkable comeback, levelling the game at 31/31, before going ahead 38/31...with only minutes to spare... England somehow, with super sub George Ford, finish the game 38/38...only a draw you say...but what a draw I say...marking one of the greatest games of rugby witnessed in six nations history.

Ireland the warriors from 2018, stumbled through match after match...not really showing us their true talent...and how many times could the Italian boys...cross the try line and not score...try after try ruled out...agonising not only for the boys on the field...but also for the mighty number of fans watching.

What a tournament...the Welsh saving their best game until the last and picking up a grand slam into the bargain...

2019 a year to look back on and tell your grandchildren about...2019 a year to analyse down the pub over a pint or three...2019 the year of the comebacks...

2019 a year to remember...

The Weeping Window

Hereford City / High Town / Church Street / Cathedral Walk,
Late snow fall covering the ground,
Follow the footsteps leading to the window display,
The radio was broadcasting, as the buzz of the town was to be unveiled.

What would we see? Only the anticipation of time would tell,
The sun shining, people gathering, a sea of tears falling,
Hundreds of poppies bringing you to a standstill on this bank holiday,
A wonder of pure delight for what they portray.

Weeping from a window high above the Cathedral grounds,
A symbol of red greeting the waiting crowds,
Each poppy resembling a life taken during the Great War,
Less we forget world war two and for what price, no one can say.

A thundering of hope falling from way, way above,
From a window so high it can almost reach the clouds,
Where spitfires once flew undercover in the dark of night,
Protecting our land from the perils that were unforeseen.

Generals, fighter pilots, foot soldiers, working men, women and children,
Taken down, shot, bombed and ripped apart,
A whole community, town, city, country turned to ash,
War does not discriminate.

Each red symbol marking a lost life…a life taken…a soul never forgotten,
Velvet red flowing, as the lady dressed head to toe, passes by,
Portraying / a grandmother, mother, sister, daughter, niece, or maybe even a widow, once someone's wife.

One hundred years, seventy years, thirty years, five years,
From two wars to save our land, up to the war on terror,
Stillness as I stand and think, bells ringing in the background,
Weeping…Weeping…Weeping…no more tears…no more fear…

…No More War.

A Memoir

(Dedicated to my late Uncle Tom, may you rest in peace)

Saturday Night

I suppose I'd better introduce myself before we start. My name is Tom; some people call me Tommy or Thomas, if I'm in trouble, as my late wife often did.

My eldest son is also called Tommy; again some people call him three different names. It's an Irish / Catholic thing. I mean naming their eldest child, after the man of the house and so forth. Not calling someone three different names, I'm sure that's not an Irish thing, even though I've been called a few choice names in my time.

Anyway I'm going off the subject, on why I've been asked to talk to you, share some of my memories and so forth. You see when you get to my age, when your wife of over forty years has passed and all your six children have grown up and fled the nest, all you have left is your memories.

Now I don't want you or anyone else feeling sorry for me. I've had a good life. My six children and twenty-four grandchildren visit me from time to time and look out for me as best they can. They all have their own families to look after; Tommy has seven for crying out loud!

Anyhow returning back to the subject in hand again. There is something that I would like to share with you all. But firstly let me tell you how this all came about.

You see, a lovely young lady called Jane came to the community centre, where I go every Wednesday for the tea and dance afternoon. It's for a bit of company you see, even though I came from a big family, the eldest of eight boys and bearing a big family myself. I still get a little lonely from time to time.

Anyway Jane introduced herself as a creative writer and asked if some of us would like to take part in a creative writing workshop. Sharing some of our own memories and developing new exciting ideas.

Well it's been a fantastic few weeks, we've had some laugh's and a few tears, dare I say. But looking over one's life, you soon realise it's not too bad, if you don't weaken.

This is the memory that I would like to share and the one good thing about reaching your later years is that you look back at things in a fond light. I hope that you all enjoy this little glimpse into my past.

....

You see it was a Saturday night. Saturday night was bath night, at the time my least favourite night of the week. But now as I am getting older, reaching the twilight years of my life and with the touch of memories, dare I say fond memories.

You see, it was a family gathering, around the open fireplace, marshmallows and hot chocolate to look forward to, after this grueling ordeal was over and done with. Now there's a memory to hold on to.

I, being the eldest would have to help my father fetch the well-worn tin bathtub from the garden shed. Mother would be boiling the giant kettle over the open flames; steam would fill the whole house.

Father would instruct us all to line up in age, the youngest first and so forth. Mother would make sure that she scrubbed us all well, behind the ears and never forgetting the neck.

Father would count us all off, one, two, three, four, five, six, seven and then finally me. I would have to sit in the same water and go through the same process, that all my brothers had just done before me.

Until finally one day I would have a bathtub of my own.

Retirement

(Dedicated to Don)

The last day of your working life seems to come around all too soon,
When your suddenly eligible for your free bus pass,
Swiftly followed by a golden handshake,
Then pension talk as we walk

Waking up the morning after the night before, please close the door,
Alarm clock no longer in use, redundant, retired just like you,
I need the loo, not once, not twice, but three times in the night,
What to do, what to do, what to do...

As the once fast, filled days, become all too slow...
Where a minute feels like an hour, an hour like a day,
A day like a week and a week like a month and with my
Annie falling asleep as I tell her about the good old days

All this spare time we now have, to look forward to,
Bingo, gardening club, whisk, washing & polishing the car,
Walking / rambling followed a pint or three,
Afternoon tea, discounted of course

Special offers and discounts galore, give me more,
Dog walking if only I had a dog?
Long days, long weeks, and even longer weekends to fill,
Where in heaven's name would you start?

Nowhere to go, nowhere to run,
Retirement reaches us all in the long run,

Be careful of what you wish for,
As old age comes knocking on the door

I'll race you to the floor, for just one more go,
Is this really the end or just the beginning?
One more slice of the cake, one more pop at the sherry,
One more knock on the door

Before I take my leave, gardening gloves at the ready,
No more rising at the crack of dawn,
Retirement plan in place,
Bowing out, as I take my place, with grace.

Racing Against Time

Darkness racing against daylight,

The waves racing against the beach,

Footsteps racing against the tide,

People racing against time,

Walkers racing against joggers,

Cyclists racing against the ramblers,

Cars racing against traffic lights,
(red, amber & green)

Dogs racing against the ball,

Wind racing against the rain,

Children racing against each other,

Horse waves racing against the shore

Spring racing against the summer,

Summer racing against autumn,

Autumn racing against winter,

Winter racing against spring,

The clocks racing against each other,

The tortoise racing against the snail,

The sun racing against the moon,

My thoughts racing against my mind,

The pen racing against the paper.

Compliment (dedicated to my dad)

It was out of character,

Lack of sleep you may think,

Or maybe the meds you say?

A long time coming,

Fifty-six years to be precise,

Out of the blue, who new!

I'm not kidding…

Mum was in disbelief and it's a good job that I was sitting down,

Mum took it in her stride,

While I remained in complete shock,

Dad went back to sleep,

Maybe it was all a dream.

Patrick Mooney - Writer and Artist

I took up creative writing just over ten years ago, specialising in poetry after becoming the first ever winner of the 'Selina Trotman' prize for poetry 2012. With my poem *The Lost Voice* (based on a true story), resulting in my first poetry book, *In a Word,* being published in 2013.

    I have been writing on a regular basis ever since and was a member of the Ledbury poetry writing group for six years. I have performed my own poetry at the Ledbury Poetry Festival and open mic nights and poetry slams in Hereford, Leominster and Cardiff.

    I have completed two travel journals, based in the USA and Europe, and a children's book, *Down on the Lake*; *Be Careful of the Falling Rocks,* is the completion of my second collection of poetry, and I am also currently developing a collection of ten short stories.

At the beginning of 2017, I thought about returning to my first creative medium art, resulting in taking on a studio at The Apple Store Gallery in Hereford, in December that same year, while continuing to write on a regular basis.

I now do all my creative writing at my studio and have completed a number of collage art works, resulting in taking on my commission last year. I also paint in acrylic, draw in pencil, in colour and black and white.

I am happy for people to contact me and would value some feedback on my new poetry collection, *Be Careful of Falling Rocks* and my creative work in general.

Contact Details:

Apple Store Gallery
www.applestoregallery.co.uk -
Open to the public (Wednesday to Friday) 10.00 to 15.00 and (Saturday) 10.00 to 13.00

Patrick Mooney - email at patrickm007@yahoo.com

Facebook at In A Word.

If you are interested in publishing, writing and you love to read, then head over to www.sleepylionpublishing.com

Otherwise, all questions can be sent to enquiries@sleepylionpublishing.com
If you would like to submit any work, whether a book, short story, article, blog post or even art work, then send us an email at submissions@sleepylionpublishing.com

We offer different paid contracts, including on smaller pieces, so whether you would rather an upfront payment, or to make money over time, we also personalise our collaborations. So, get in contact now and start earning money from your work!

On our website you will find:

-Our personal editing, illustrating and publishing services
- Blog posts
 -Articles on writing and reading
-Essays (coming soon)
-Short Stories
-Book Covers
-Poetry
-Exciting Merchandise
-Range of different non-binding contracts
-News on any books we are publishing

www.ingramcontent.com/pod-product-compliance
Lightning Source LLC
Chambersburg PA
CBHW071533080526
44588CB00011B/1656